DATE DUE

AP 12 '96			
MY 7 '98			

DEMCO 38-296

NOVA

NOVA

POEMS BY BARON JAMES ASHANTI

HARLEM RIVER PRESS

New York City

NOVA IS DEDICATED TO MY
CHILDREN
MARCUS KWAZI ASHANTI
AND
NOVA AKOSUA ASHANTI
AND ALSO
BRENDA
THE LITTLE RAVEN

————————————

TABLE OF CONTENTS

NUBIANA

NOVA

The author would like to acknowledge the support and encourage-
ment of Marie Dutton Brown.

Some of the poems in the present volume have appeared in the follow-
ing magazines and quarterlies: *Nethula II*; *Hoodoo VII*; *Blacks on Paper
III*; *Blacks on Paper IV*;
Essence Magazine; *Kalimba*; *Afro-Realism*; *New Heat*; *Greenfield
Review*; *Indigene*; *Obsidian*; *Through The Looking Glass*; and *Pavan*

NOVA

BARON JAMES ASHANTI is a new brightness for an age of shadows. but the irradiance that he brings to the creative scene is not innocent or uninitiated light. "B.J." has traveled over vast reaches of the spirit, and his chronology of contributions to the legacy of African-American poetry goes back to the stirring 1960s.

His style has moved in his travels from a sometimes tumbling outpouring of *Negritude* cadences to the controlled, ideologically charged fusillade of this present work — this *Nova*.

Nova is a book of heroes, heroines, and heroic resistances set in jewel-like works propelled by rocket-fuel energies and a romantic imagination. The prime impulse of the volume is to celebrate legendary figures who have transformed our perceptions of human possibilities through poetry, art, and song. The ideology of the book is that of an oxymoron: tenderness and caring can make a difference if one is sufficiently informed and significantly revolutionary. The dynamics of the ideology spell themselves out in the many poems dedicated to the poet's children, in the utterances of sincere concern for their safety in a Hiroshima universe, and in the adulation to the contours of their bodies and the infinity of their developmental promise. The tougher complement to such sentiment is scathing denunciation of pimp-walking MBAs teetering on the corporate ladder, or bitter sarcasm directed at Dame Liberty in her relationship to Chinese students or South African freedom fighters.

But *Nova's* signal brightness (as I have already hinted) is not a revolutionary light — no matter how tempered by personal familiar involvements. *Nova's* first brightness lies in its engagement of the poet's sensibilities with the sense and sensuousness of the lives of creators such as Mozart, Picasso, Sterling Brown, Aimé Césaire, and so many others. It is in the "portrait poems" that Baron James Ashanti seems to invest his intimate energies — and they sing or explode with emotion. They represent the poet in his most committed public voice.

Yet, after a poem precisely about "transition" in *Nova,* we witness the poet's shift to lyrical transformation of landscapes of personal experience. "New York Fugue" joins that American host of "city poems" that carry us past familiar names and territories and transforms them in the office of the poet's own great adventures of the human soul. *Nova's* post-transition poems strive — sometimes with a mighty self-consciousness — for control of both the poet's interior world of emotion and this emotional world's standing with respect to the urban experience.

The place of *Nova* in the archives of contemporary poetry and in the canons of African-American poetry is certainly with multi-syllabled activists such as Neruda, Hayden, Tolson, and continental and Caribbean figures such as Senghor and Césaire.

The very prodigality of B.J. Ashanti's visions, dreams and vocabularies indicate that *Nova* is not only signal brightness among us, but a *new* star, a beginning that augurs a continuing genius of words.

In many ways *Nova* is both a blessed book and a blessing among us.

Dr. Houston A. Baker, Jr
Philadelphia, Pennsylvania
January, 1990

THE MUSIC

JAZZ SINGER
— IF JAZZ BE A LADY
HER NAME BE BETTY CARTER

Sienna buttocks of the stage
flesh wrinkled soft under spotlight

where lady slender close to microphone
gestures a pain — sensual as strength
casts slivers of melody
to splint evening's chasm

She sings as winsome cherry
swallowing tears in the pit of reason . . .

the crowd wants more !

JAZZ SONG

Tilt of the apple-jack
amputates a thousand dreams from their moorings

as the Harlem River floats in the doorway
like lips singing thick lightning
on tips of spiral shadows
where syncopated limbs dance the blues

ain't nothing but a song
talking 'bout limbo and waters forgetting
the subtle taste of coral

ain't nothing but a tear in this sea
talking 'bout limbo
a dance full of blues /

A HOOFER'S TALE
FOR BILL "BOJANGLES" ROBINSON

Bojangles miscast
in role of neutered darkie
sentenced to celluloid chain gang
where troubled soul hustled
tin cup & saloon tract
with nickel & dime dexterity

wretched survival at any cost
bought by series of flying bucks
in urban landscapes that coined
seduction by rhythm & sound
while every musical tone from
shoe taps was a tear
choreographed by copacetic rage
projecting antebellum image
across racism's profit margin /

Bojangles
De Mayor ah Harlem's off screen
temperament as pistol packing
affirmation behind "tom" facade

the living contradiction
between art & reality !

EXCERPT FROM
THE NEW MUSIC

Hungry shriek of a saxophone
left out in the four winds
sum total of the middle passage

truth lays only in visions of madmen
muted solo of warriors wrapped in rags
cold
a Black woman blanket swallowed
on Gimbels' steps . . .
hazel eyed nod with
cigarette between lips
ashes falling on tits
below oboe scratching snowflakes and sunshine;

a fire to warm our hands when tears work roots !

DUET
FOR MY SON MARCUS

From wandering urgency
city streets screened technicolor
we confluent stride to commensurate
tensile strength endowed by inheritance
that simple act of breathing myth
called The Blues

We blow and draw
dyad stroke and climb scaffolding
of musical scales testing our licks
methodology of harmonica wheeze
mimics infant's rage
you the bawling bundle in my arms
sit now in my lap
you say "show me daddy"

arm's crook defines hug in my smile
wishing that I knew more to teach
we struggle on together
father & son
harps in hand
small triumphs to chiseled mouths
as tin and wood stretch life
into the images of ourselves
magic notes so blue / black & perfect
you'll understand my love
when you hear the song /

SOUTHERN CROSS
FOR JANIS JOPLIN

Trouble ferrying loneliness
through chords stitching devil's music
sounds of vibrant colors
minor 5th stutters-love sick & horny
thick body writhe-tantrum stomp
heart rending song
familiar crime scene disconsolate passions
where cracker gal lost
in moonlit shards' forest
honed voice into awesome weapon
throat as cyclops . . .
second sight
on china berry's lilac flame /

Sawdust in air
with whiskey's heavy shot
while she slow dragged with heartache
during perpetual midnight
the pain wasn't new
but J.J. could've been anybody
she wanted
when she sang The Blues !

JUST ANOTHER GIG
FOR CHARLIE PARKER

Rampaging spectral images
darkling strange & imminent
marathon fingers vamping
base chords while 16th note diatribe
focuses like needling rain
trips but never falls
the melody is troublesome
cross-fire of musical notes
running changes from needle's ambrosia
quick-fix for demi-god gypsy flight
on main-line rhythms / be-bop liturgy
with Bird on point
when passion be trial by ordeal
feeding on vanity of the riff

under spotlight constellations
cutting session be like corner fight
with Prussian blue straight razors
urban tragedy of feeling too much
becomes inimitable art
in this civet smelling nocturnal world
audiences set on edge
by stubborn beauty of pain
and here
incompetence be the only enemy /

Hunched shoulders as venue
for monster probe
millennium journey of nights on
tracks in arms
be map of terrible country
whistle-stop tours
endless roll call of nameless dives
road song which tempts with perdition's justice
when immortality be flagrant as pungent sex

on & on
tension ramrod strict
where he is always here
just beyond reach &
brilliance just another
walk-on role /

Legend of the alto's bell
shooting star across life's brocaded tapestry
and cigarette smoke clouds
soar in wild geese formation
when the moon flat-lines midnight skies
something sad illuminates our memory
as we grieve his absence;

rogue cunning stalking future shock
the void a step into the unknown !

CASCADES
FOR SCOTT JOPLIN

When an ivory moon deals aces
from honky-tonk shadows
soft shoe twilight will dance
with band box precision
top hat in hand and toothy grin
steps where musical notes are guides
to handsome women's company

dressed in nightgowns of sweat and lusty laughter
as red lights cook down in the Tail Gates
hothouse of flesh brews like fast moonshine
cold cash can buy satin vice of raven hued thighs
Joplin — sporting house professor
bent over piano keys
draws to royal flush;

if you touch his soul
music will turn into a pearl of black smoke
blown by Mississippi breezes whispering
slanted visions that walk with a cane
such a fine madness the heart will say
that a tambourine
cakewalks and simmers in a glass of blue wine /

When tiers of rain greet the heart
songs will taste like bourbon
tempo will strut measure for measure
like autumn cockleburrs punctuating
city pavement's script
where itinerant musicians starve

Joplin threw clenched fists through staff and bar
listen to the nail against slate
Joplin as renegade and penniless
while posterity exploits his genius

but he is more — so much more
than rancor and the North Wind's sterile ear /

JAMAICA

BUSRIDE

De trip 'ome look
look like a map a ra city
weh bag carry-come
life day ta day
widow ha sorrow — she man garne
by weh ha mechanical claw
rollin' t'rough night
wid street 'allowed out enna darkness

she man garne by weh ha 'unger
limbs drawn like t'read ha weave
ha barren love —
weh she survive an' de scent escape
de scar on har flank weh time beat har
mudder ah Blackness
har pickney dem snatched from har womb
but dem mem'ry suckle from limp breasts
weh she shows har nipple ha molten razors

she ride bus an' gwon say taste
she take she love an' get on
weh autumn ride rhythms de weh ha snakes
Bus Stop !

She people stare an' wonder why
she 'ad to be a nigger
she take she love an' get awn wid tot'less anger
weh she tongue taste blood
an' curse she chil'ren's ignorance
deir vogue ha remiss

deir 'atreds ha roots
an' blood line dat curve like monument
just so
she take she word — let 'em fall
muh ticulous in deir acid like thick squall
in de face ha she pickney dem lie
she pickney dem ride de damn bus
day laugh when she say storm
Bus Stop !
Enna runs in har stockin's
like tough stain de weh she 'urts
she cry
she say "it pains so"
"Lawd" she say, "remember de smell ha cane
an' de weh pickney came to be once ?"
She pickney dem ride bus
say "par . . . ty" an' smell gin
"Remember," she say "de spirit prancin'
lak ha sex ha revenge in de eye ha de sun
an' de Blackness dat drank de sun ?"

And she say "all y'all gonna die
eena yer 'igh 'eels . . .
y'all got no respect fer life !"

She pickney dem ride bus next to har
look at she 'eart
and say "she crazy !"

VERSION
FOR BOB MARLEY

Vogue the splendor as Seaga
curses Rasta but calls him hero
John Crow them a wear suit
and pass law fer we
but Ruddy play tough and live
and that's a good Ruddy-Ruddy /

Killing zone the praise
more than absence
flesh as army of words
maroon erect angle stride
this brown agate storm-justified called man

bass drum lion's pulse into song
where revolution walks rock stone
as tiger-ram
streets aflame when music's rhythm
smiles with penny wauli eyes

smoke curls for line portrait
while the spiff burns like a copper moon
against blue bath of midnight sky
embers become a shower of falling stars
that glimmer in the sea as island
oh island eternal

Edward Seaga, a former Prime Minister of Jamaica

Iree here Locksman !

The diurnal star wears a mask
of hittite iron and down the cheeks
a stream of elegant tears infiltrates
the dream spun terror of nationhood

Struck like a bloody gem
Prestor John's duppy alliance
forms legions that arm themselves
in the mountain swell of rebellious charm
and Marley's legacy
walks the blue cobalt sea
with infinite grace /

John Crow, Jamaica, large scavenger bird
Taggoram, Jamaica, large male goat
Penny Wauli, Jamaica, fire fly
Spiff, Jamaica, cigar-size marijuana cigarette
Prestor John, Jamaica, mythical Ethiopian emperor
Duppy, Jamaica ghost

THE OLD SOLDIERS
FOR THE WW I & WW II VETERANS
OF PORT ANTONIO, PORTLAND,
JAMAICA

With the weeping saga of memory's colon
peppered with cannon shot conflicts echo
hammer against manacle in scar tissue's trench

as clouds of spines trek
in the form of mustard gas
and no one remembers the battle
but oh . . . the legend of bright medals
the glory contagious !
After ceremony
reality is the taste of salt
his strong back just a means to survive
down in the pock marked Earth
him breathing bauxite dust
where freedom is colony of purpose

years auctioned off
with husky voice of bitter trade winds
chastising pearl embossed mountains
stacked in the sky like silent guardians
burnished by gloaming's velvet hand /

Ah time . . .
evangelic witch as faithless consort
of seclusion and the work ethic's fiction
changes men
makes them hungry

Ah time . . .
    time I tell you

an ignorant man must be a poor man . . . yes ?
and he was young
his Avalon a tramp steamer
packed with a volley of colonial subjects
fired point blank at England's destiny

From the provinces
local color pawned by penitentiary's shadow
carried in a carnival of brown paper grips

and that day wore a bandage of gull's wings
the docks flooded by urgency
the smell of desperate travel
about this immigrant army bloodied
by a system of breaking stations

and this young man's tomorrows
like so many others'
ransomed off for coolie wages
and a second world war fought
to save the British Crown

he accepted a homebound convenant
past a wharf of loneliness
where hasty decisions get their end away /

Ah time . . .
    time and its bald spot
with dreams a swamp of matted hair
and reeds of festering sores
lined with a symphony of chattering maggots
stranded in 'see-me-no-more gully'
and the drama of the stand pipe draws
the day's news from the heat of necessity
as thick as toto /

The old man now a crutch
that holds up the hill with a cement skeleton
of a house waiting on this year's additional rib —
perhaps a wife's room

"Doan crush up mi pockets mon
me did never marry you know
mi caan afford fi 'ave woman
a pretty wife needs a pretty house !"

The years come and gone so
like a summer storm
Jamaica sovereign now mon yes
celebrating independence draws the old soldiers
with their bow ties

Toto, a Jamaican potato pudding

garrisoned around sunrise
with its frayed collar
damp with horizon's sweat

their skin passed on to whit leather
covering brittle bones folded over
weathered benches in the square

a game of checkers helps them catch the sun
before the young ones "jump up"

the old ones move too slowly now
for current events
but the tiger plantain still holds lechery
in its one eye . . .

these old ones
whetstone of a nation's history
in their souls

them ah hurt
but them proud . . . boy . . .
but them ah proud !

MUSGRAVE MARKET
FOR THE PEOPLE OF PORT
ANTONIO, JAMAICA

A guinea-hen scratching for corn
kicks pebbles through arid textures
another day letting sunlight bleed
from Saturday's lacerations

Day morning well paid before Jesus
the sea a painted gypsy
outline of hills touching sky
tender like a woman's pleasure spread wide
under a dress' flower print canopy
bathed in a barefoot breeze that blows
toward town sweetly in search of commerce
she . . . a strapping woman strides the road
carrying the world of her family's survival
on her head . . . breadfruit, pimento, ganips

She /
    / them
long legged bodies in short peasant skirts
breaking waves of heat rising from morning's breath
like hope flowing down the road as lava . . .
an aged hand leaning on a staff
the dirt road rippling in concentric circles
claiming offspring with definite authority
of wounded syllables strung together like pearls /

The heat of necessity draws them
with their tough smiles
and rum fractured dreams
to a galvanized anthill of a building

squat and dark where morning
chews the business of buying and selling
with teeth of stark white sugar cane /

Sun-hot
and the skull of this anthill
filled with the pantheon of anarchy
the drone of tourists attacking dignity
adapt in their ignorance like flies to cowshit

and the heat of necessity binds people
like coconut thatch into a blanket of strength

binds them to the day
house in the pungent scent of raw trade
enclave of jerk-pork and daylight
diffused through slits for eyes of this skull /

The anthill's mouth inundated
with mahogany tides that purify streets with life
where the town's fool dance / walks
slapping his chest to the pulse
of Reggae sun rhythms
winding off the waist of the town

as ragtag children hungry for truth
follow the idiom of promise in the fool's innocence
follow beyond blue stripe policeman's swagger
whose preponderant sway of arm
against pistol forgets people
but remembers subjects to authority

"move, move on !"
he says

And the heat of necessity
draws children to cheer the fool's ragged defiance
and the roots
and the dance that celebrates life
past blue stripe hooligan's strife
and the skull of the anthill drinks their laughter
like thirsty Earth /

In late afternoon a swirl of colors
dilated by sunbeams dying in cracks
of the zinc skull of anthill
are caught in the higgler's net of words

"de point fah life bwoy is soil
dem straw basket look pretty-pretty
wit dem yellow fleshed yawn of ackee
dem pulp eye lookin' a pear green breeze
dat wars wit de heat ha necessity
an de fragrance ha chocolate tea confuse de issue . . .
de point fah life is soil !"

Musgrave Market women with their
neeseberry breasts suckling a nation
fighting against assigned destiny
these women water the soil with vaginal mist
which gathers on flowers made from hands
molding quietude of fruition
that grows in a vineyard of wooden stalls
planted in the skull of this anthill of activity

This Saturday digested where capsized stools
become markers for lives
and Musgrave Market Women carry the future
back to the bush-bush as evening sighs
with a gush of Jamaican starlight /

URBAN CLIMES

STARSTRUCK
FOR FRANCES FARMER, MARILYN MONROE, AND JEAN SEBERG

During an age of fabulous fedoras
film studios held scavenger hunts
for rave reviews through snake-pit bramble
where one's life became public spectacle
foul images' tantrum filtered
through gossip column rumor
and there were golden girls
bright eyed and fresh pilgrims

backwater sylvan assailed by bizarre flight from poverty
steered toward exploitive Saxon rite of siege . . .
lifetimes embroidered with sensible shoes —
simple, sweet, and kind things idled
by glamor's aura where casting couch lint
hung from scripts' widowed lines . . .
bucking crosswinds of Hollywood starlets
haunt this pesthole democracy
creates darlings' forms
human sacrifice amid soft core rubble
the girl next door as sodom-hipped trinket /

Above the secular din of mortal pestilence
where male chauvinism's bestial alchemy
with its cruel mission sought to transform
sparkling universe engendered by womens' bodies
into biological warfare; this conflict
of anatomical parts as laissez faire commerce
in the flesh trade

misbegotten legacy
directors, leading men, talent scouts
hot on the trail of sexual conquest
when a millennium of miscarriages and
backroom abortions
minted new genre of suffering
the camera inclined toward scandal
body-english becomes wet pavement reflections
of some pin-up queen's tarnished life . . .
crack mirrored seams leaking deadly illusions

in the end
tinsel town's femmes fatales ride gilded frost
that drifts from gun metal meadow of a T.V. set
as late show specters in the form
of ivy branch portraits
backlit by an obscenely beautiful full moon's lantern;

every girl's dream . . . perhaps !

AN URBAN PASTORAL

Central Park after dark
call sign / wilding
cloven attitude
of seeds as cannibals
familiar breakdown
this pathology of neglect
everyone's fault
but our own
the Black middle class
solid in its
distinguished weakness
the old ways
of dignity, self respect
& kindness lost to the
pursuit of happiness &
the god almighty dollar bill /

Anatomy of heinous crime
gang rape as media event
trial by error
fury of stone in glass-house
where reservation
pried loose by wolf pack
of rampaging Black youth
fear the crop
for springtime harvest !

PEEP SHOW
A PORTRAIT OF A TOPLESS DANCER

Ruthless lust staggers up to brass rail
chameleon like man set adrift in clothes
lost between years where he leers
at long legged sadness semi nude
flurrys of bumps and grinds
doing a Murphy Game — anaemic roving blood
of singapore-slings . . .

this sable woman's belly rub hides twice the pain
cesarean scarred memory & hard times
a lady in ruby satin whose sex laden movements
binds wounds of colonized longings
cause all they'll ever have is a good woman
and she belongs to them tonight /

Coerced —
she does what has to be done
motherhood trapped in voyeur's sweatshop
this bimsha's star rises $15 an hour
erotic premise — enveloped by
wall of mirrors and chased by cat-calls

"Somebody hold me !" she pleads
stems of her flower
outstretched limbs
an eminent black orchard . . .

she closes her eyes and pretends love
is more than commodity of liquid flesh
hawking phantasies staining "g" string

with steel drum melodies in tropic loneliness
spotlights & stale cigarette smoke /

Bimsha, Caribbean, starkly beautiful dark-skinned Black woman

THE NATIVITY OF
THE ODYSSEY BAR & GRILL

Bad Foot Jimmy sings a field holler
courting sand papered voice
from the bottom of a shot glass in the bar . . .

swing-blade rhythm against the Harlem sky
with sunset called Black Magic
hound dogs barking and thunder tracing
steps of smoke that move in whirlpools
across the levee of his past
where he . . . Bad Foot Jimmy sings to frustration
of neon eyelids blinking
at a wine bottle green moon
and night gauche with passion

blood boiling in a sex
of back alley hotels where Crazy Mary
is burnt to a crisp by experience
and flirts with love
under sunset called Black Magic /

The wind as anarchy and this lady's eye
– yes – reminds one
of a river of clairvoyant stars
breaking against the profuse fragrance
of clover and honey

and
yet

once this woman a pleasure
hand to mouth mantra of mint
laid under tongue
now with neurotic shocks of the womb
stretched to receive sins
from 2 generations of faithless lovers

a sunset called Black Magic

retraces experience of topsoil
moist beneath surface as spawn of men
crawl from weathered cracks in her skin

just a little sport
and tonight's erection sandwiched between
the sweet folds of her need
a bedbug infested mattress and dirty sheets
the memory of mama's mahogany breakfront
and Crazy Mary . . . a child . . . safe

remember
a wood fire burning sweetly
posed as a barrier against harm

and
yet

when it's over the scene dissolves
into hospital bleached corridors
a tear

and Crazy Mary's hand jerks like static electricity
scratching invisible sores always present
in greasy spoon restaurants
in bed with lovers
in terror
in a place where hurt becomes a special crop
that transforms her 47 years
into grinding hips of a 20 year old chippy

and
yet

even repeated burying
of scorpion's sting
in hull of womb can bear fruit

"jelly
jelly
jelly . . . jelly on my mind
jelly killed my father
it drove my mother stone blind . . ."

And a bump and grind stutters
like drunken two step
hysteria leaps from her womb
like prancing iguanas
in flight from invading footsteps

in secret territory
the heart–yes–more than orgasm
more than hope

and Crazy Mary . . .
breasts ripe with milk
cries in disbelief of beauty
to be some child's mother
after all these years
she cries as if Bad Foot Jimmy's song
is personal /

The spirit is a needle like mist
falling as pieces of a dream
"see I was loved once !"
30 years old love letters testify
always present

Crazy Mary on a bar stool
floods her tight dress
wet with miscarriage's benediction

this classic beauty up from southern lowlands
cottonhead blow against the odds
losing
but ah . . . to have tried is another matter

This madonna and child dying
like a simpering whisper
gripped by savage timbales . . .
so much warmth put to rest
with so little love . . .
        another time
        another life)

A SMALL MIRACLE

August guided
by a shower of light years' scatter-shot
when evening clothed in Black antique satin skin
spooned sensual heat wafting like incense
below metabolic rage of the zodiac's asylum
attracting a
veve of thunder and shooting stars
written across the sky
sounding a chorus of angry tenor saxophones
as I walked between breath of fallen angels' wings
thick toward midnight's far side
during relentless agony of a city
that cares in irregular shifts

this civil war of human wonder
summoned walking death to hustle artifacts
from conjugal nightmares of drug cordoned ruins

predatory street
smelling of burning cinders
and
forced to steal bad habits
waiting for signs
and a blue funk's jubilee streamed my blood

In the shadow of a church
under street lamp-full moon an altar defined conjure's
def rap
as it packed some deacon's dilemma

a votive summer breeze
with intoxicated affect
whispered
to white candle warm lilt
on loa's meal smothered in onions
while catered cigar & rum
rounded after dinner discussion

This altar
an unselfish invocation
for community under siege
evil spirits and zombies familiar
but
that night
my street could not find the abyss

Veve. In the religion of Voodoo, a drawing made from flour used for
specific effect-drawing of a spirit (loa) to conjure good luck, etc.

Loa, Yoruba, local deity

THE RUMBLE

The day's kettle boiled
and cutrate horror summoned
afternoon sunshine to throw a spotlight
on the drug inspired greenhouse affect that
wrapped itself around stacked angry streets
& the ghetto's daily grind
like a scintillating curtain of heat

while pieces & snatches
of hustler's prattle fell
like premature autumn leaves
where most things
except despair grow with difficulty

chances rare
the deck rigged
like some gambler's nightmare
and childhoods evaporate
into dire race for survival /

Shuffled
into natural order
an uneasy quiet descended
causing
tenement bricks, innocent by-standers
and ancillary props to tense up
as if some common reflex had taken hold
the moment frozen in time . . .

and then suddenly
it happened . . .
a stampede of shadow flesh darted
up the street's middle core
and formed into a gang of Black youth
who stopped on a dime
turned on their heels
waiting for inevitable showdown

within heartbeat's span
a second volley of blurred images
in multi rhythmic formation
dodged ambush
these young ram cutthroats, thieves,
and butchboy teenagers

manoeuvred with tactical aplomb
in full view of witnesses

and threw
fusillades of pies at each other
tired of fratricide & slaughter
laughter replaced bullets
and good old fashioned fun
soaked the street that day
instead of tears & blood !

MUSEUM PIECE

A green blanket marks the battle
a discarded living person who haunts
cold concrete horrors of midtown
by dawn's early light
a particular sadness wells in the eye
as sky purports innocuous day
a miracle stepping out of time
the sun's transparent flask of molten ceruse
poured over a morning which bristles
with those who live out on the streets
and smell of what is most wrong in America . . .

opaque journey of sandwichboard economy
which aches with pleas from these urban gypsies
direct from central casting — sitting & waiting
patient to the point of perversion's jagged edge
these cross legged entities
with walking canes & civilized torments
their disturbing presence of broken rail's deportment
as shards from decayed flesh
peal beneath statistics & soiled shopping bags

inmates of Grand Central Station's roost
where crow's feet jump double-dutch from cold
these denizens of rembrandt hues
speak an unfamiliar dialect of shadows
which seek to cope with a willingness to need

and wisdom is weighed by incoherence
manic courage is mustered by communal wine
a feeble libation poured
from this human croft of the human will
and shuffled between rush / hour daydreams

The trap drum's iambic pulse dances
slopes of high hat cymbals
all day and into the nighttime sepulcher
I tried to figure out this pressure cooker
that destroys beauty — and here we are
the only slaves on Earth with golden chains
this American soap opera which creates
sociopaths, burn / outs and volunteers
for victimhood as national past / time !

Better deforming pain than empty pockets
in New York's lagoon of shark grey concrete . . .

Uptown morne
at working day's end
a lapidary's fine touch etches abstract forms
into human traits
endowed with legendary conservatism
reeking of christian dogma & camphor liniment

Morne, Martinique, a Black ghetto

velvet last of sephardic night
offering sanctuary from silver throat pharisees
whose technocracy renders images boiler / room exercise
which stokes inner city into sweltering holocaust
corner bar as bantustan sucks up on karma
surrounded by moist & nubile shot / glass fantasies
dancing semi / nude

I stumbled home without having taken a step
frightened by the feel of being a relic
drunk with nostalgia
that most dangerous of drugs
I bolted a maze of raindrops
to join an ambuscade of off duty janitors & laborers
walking harlem's wet streets like zombies

It was 3 a.m. /tired of drink I mourned
the absence of truth & answers which were final

A RECENT MADNESS

Elm and white pine in full bloom
worn
down
to textures of attrition's blight
while spring shower's frenzy
ushers office workers in & out of shelter
as if they were game board pieces

rented court jesters
illustrious pawns
would-be mistresses
& drones who shine
corporate banisters with wiggling asses

misplaced haughtiness
distorts any semblance of truth
where shit doesn't stink
this adjectival excess endemic
to park bench sideshow
of blistering human conditions
grey this grim urban gothic
whose broken logic chases its own tail
— and it's feeding time at the zoo —

And here he comes like clockwork
Yeshiva graduate of green eye revelry
lost in sediment of messenger boy's serfdom
he had it all
and all of it should've been enough
but it got lost and went to seed

The noon break's white knuckled dialectic
extends beneath abandoned symmetries
of patrician features which have gone into hiding
— his Brahman colored face — as moiré surface
rippling reflective anger as he stalks
Rittenhouse Square flailing air wildly
arms too weak to lift failure's burden
he is still mulvein believer in a caste system
left to its own devices as flotsam from another era

Walk Over
Walk Over

as he rambles
he rumbles — his libretto of despair
preaching out loud
to the host of personalities inside
his intemperate rage that resists
cruel pressures in maintaining his job
at any cost and against all odds
and for his trouble
makes jello out of human mind

And now Brother Sunshine's tantrum
poses low down edification
for professional elite sitting on benches
imbued with brown bag pragmatism
they watch and laugh

Mulvein, Afro-American, a Black person so light of color that the blue
of his or her veins is visible

at the gadfly with
elephantine limbs
spastic movement
and a poet's eye . . .

The lunch hour dissolves — acid on silk —
and sanity takes hold on schedule
at that precise moment when reality
tugs against the seams of his wallet
back to work
that miraculous smile in place
and murder on the brain

Walk Over
Walk Over !

THE INTERNATIONAL

HIROSHIMA BLUES
FOR MARCUS & NOVA ASHANTI

doomsday lullaby for modern era
tonight my small children sleep and dream
of toys and kindhearted mischief
but what if . . .
the everlasting headache resounded
against walls of a crematorium for rational thought
when survival's techniques go nova —

deafening silence
and then tell-tale flash
as sky becomes dayglow wonder
fire-storms ripping flesh from civilization

my children's comrades incinerated
or if they lived
curse of walking dead
bodies lacerated with black rain
bones polished smooth
by radiation's smile
could my son and daughter survive
would I see them again ?

A sad symphony of flamenco guitars
and lamenting violins and cellos wretch tears
from a cache of rad
larger than imagination's wildest torment
this "Strangelove" serenade of
a geiger counter's rabid castanet's

click
click
click
click
hard times for this promethean gulag called Earth
where cowl robbed mutant choir glows
in cave dark fallout's fray singing chants
for humanity's last vestige

these victims of war without bullets
this hair-triggered shudder
where thermo nuclear fire-balls slam dance
in memory plagued by grade b scripts
while prune faced Reagan dozes in the oval office
corporate dons direct america
into an arms race no one can win /

Megaton madness-profit margin's mushroom cloud
as devil seed sprouting rigid textures
and the Pentagon's evil creed cannibalizes
social progress to fuel
world imperialism's fetid war machine
unemployment lines overflow
and national priorities become obscured
by billions for "defense"
bread not bombs the world's populations protest . . .

and through it all
my sweet daughter and son sleep
and I worry will I ever see them again !

SALOME

Bonded burnt umber as human sacrifice
beautiful and gift wrapped
she gyrates for technocrats
while primal seduction of power
provides music-methodic and alluring
her veils of restraint pealed
by prevailing winds of nuclear madness

and on she dances

where Chernobyl waits for us all
this civilized terror endured
for rank progress' sake
in a world too small to contain secrets
the stubborn rote of cynicism
enticed the Kremlin
to play hide and seek as they
stone-walled the Communist Manifesto
the party-line betrayed
the true courage of the Soviet
and the world's wide eyed socialists
were left to struggle with the weight
of their own idealism
stranded in the lurch of political expediency /

Kremlin hedonism factored into state paranoia
with
May Day on the brink of holocaust
speak no evil
hear no evil

laughing eyes terror stricken and blinded
by hunger and the atom's revenge

and on she dances

with nude writ of discovery
beckoning patriarchal lust . . .
sex object of our wildest dreams

As Freud's vindication battles
for the championship of the bloomin' world —
best 2 falls out of 3 !

BEIJING SPRING

I
A sea of scarlet banners
punctuated a new page of history
written by whirlwind patriots

in the Year of The Snake
the peoples' will must succeed
doing a freedom dance right to left
the dialectical process struggled
under another harsh daybreak
and sunbeam spikes nailed the coffin
of misplaced authority
as Tianamen Square convulsed in protest
where wisteria leafed brooms swept
 bureaucratic malfeasance;

The Gang of Elders
forgot the meaning
and true fervor of passion
martial law failing
to control higher forms of order !

II
Stroke /
    / counter-stroke
a net of rust catches the horizon's shadow
The Long March perjured and buried beneath
menstrual ash as it deserts Mao's triumph
now safe behind legend and under house arrest
augurs ill of China

Uneven reform is a road
only traveled by the fool
hybrid government beyond the sun
unable to lead by broken faith
controls people's will by force
tears of blood as storm's water in air
during heartbreak dawn
livid with staccato applause
which littered streets with crushed bodies
of martyred students and workers
shot down by the hundreds

Revolution does not come
by default wrapped neatly
in a shroud of Mandarin elegance

in war innocence is the first casualty
murder of the innocent cannot bring honor
to those who claim victory

the mist of teardrops shrieks
with a peal of events where
the mountain breeze tied with bamboo silk
is nothing more than process /

And human bonfires lit the way
to death strewn harvest
the helpless
the unarmed
with only
a moment to change a life forever

Official rhetoric cannot ease tragedy
this circus of emotions
where destiny is carnivorous

and mothers wait in vain
for children to return

and oh . . .
whatever happened to
The White Haired Girl ?

June 1989

White Haired Girl. A revolutionary Chinese ballet whose protagonist
is a symbol of the aspirations of common people in triumph against the
forces of oppression.

III
Revolution is the legacy of youth
human spirits evolved toward better selves
but in China these sad days
pounding heartbeats' shudder race bullets' impact
during concurrent drama of denied hope

savaged ideal cocoon emerges in panoramic horror
world witnessed blood lunacy
this revisionist lie which edits history
with cold hand and empty heart
to elicit bad penny's karma /

China
a nation as wave of flesh suppressed
land of slaughtered lambs
during this festival of dream-thought
pitched to frenzy

they had no reason to fear authority
the future had always been promised to them
and as they sang The International
patriotic song blistered the ear of dour cynicism

mass arrests, executions and misery
where ideology is supposed to divine
better life
but . . .
the buried skeleton of truth
strengthens the soil;
there is no other reality !   *July 1989*

EPILOGUE — THE U.N. PLAZA

Life & death as gyre of change
this hard headed litany
with the poet's eye as mosaic of mirrors
that reflect new moon stain
rubbed over social evolution that
draws sustenance from
human condition's continental wheeze

as masses gather in an urban swelter
where humidity of passions erupt
beyond gates of race & culture
dynastic parasites' feudal rule
fueled by "heaven's mandate" or stale ideology
ignites geometry of world protest
common biology sipping brooding wine
of neolithic tears — bullets against hope

and I am there
and I am there

Ten years ago in The Plaza
my fist full of poems' voice thundered
against Reverend Dr. Tolbert's rice monopoly
& starvation courted Liberia's general populace
hundreds gunned down in the name
of an elite's fetid avarice . . .
beyond its flag
does a country belong to the people ?

The Statue of Liberty
once a celebration of freed
American slaves
but reality
stuck up under apartheid's wings . . .
where the terror of Bensonhurst racism poses quandary
for American dreams — the scales of justice
rigged like a crooked pawn broker's assay

The Lady in The Harbor's tears
peeled flakes
of municipal lime green tarnish
from her robes
and they flew on wings of sea salt
to Soweto, and Beijing as seeds . . .

The sad necessity of a decade's cycle
attracted my voice
and I stood in The Plaza once again
much grayer but stronger & confident
in the grand protocol of art
serving the fallen
as each poem became character reference
for humanity
beyond neglect's forgetfulness
and a young Chinese woman on hunger strike
clutched my poems in her fist
as spring rain illustrated collective grief /

All of us belong to Mother Earth
believe in freedom's struggle
commit or perish !

PORTRAITS

DUENDE
FOR PABLO PICASSO

Scourge if nothing more
than a song of blood
gushing forth in venal appetite for the immortal

Your hour of triumph brings
slaughter for apathiques
and vengeful justice to dilettantes . . .

A chorus of furies chant the drama
of stroke and contour's flow
as torment for mode through mood
when limbs like wire shrink / now grow
to measure the world

by the soul's passion —
images vault from nightmare's atelier
out Picasso's open window and petals
from turpentine bouquet creates
on the wall's other side
turtledoves that coo like Picasso's children;

things become calm and life begins
in his eyes savage glare
that dawned sunrise probing reality
beyond senses as piss colored fandango

Duende, Spanish folklore, the creative demon of genius

Oh power profane
Picasso the invader with fever
of Andalusian guitars guided by comet's brilliance
El Maestro as warlock of sensitive touch
mates with la femme
la femme
whose hair of flagellating eel chastises
tradition into moaning impotence
la femme
whose features have gone awry
nipples pour milk from armpits;

a mouth that speaks both coming and going
dribbling queues of liquid pearl
from oral conquest
her swiftly curved body as voracious predator
    runs
    lays
grunts / humps
wildly in perpetual motion . . . ah . . .

She swarms to primed canvas
summoned by fingers that nimble-clutch
the brush which speaks with language
of falling leaves for delicate altitude
ingesting with pale hunger
a brackish sky's autumn tears that lap
ochre sand and the human skull's black & grey cliffs /

Duende comes to devour the artist
with gravel laden siren's voice
perfumed with hypnotic rhythms
darting from a garrison of textured hues
for hope
for defiance

the demon shifts & quakes a painter's life
he who pursues the dreamscape romance
of bizarre likeness

stigma / erect angle through
color prism breaks to azure mysticism
virility gives way to sweat's isolation
when vast perspectives meander-gleam
to abstract form and body mass /

Strip the composition clean
and genius will smile with death's knowledge
as failure of excess taints weeping sunset
mauve and pink when ennui's puntilla
stab the minotaur with jealous rage

moment of truth's confession
blurred with flashing steel — the bullfight
predestined / the demon satiated . . . bon soir
                    bon soir
                    Picasso /

RIFF FOR AMADEUS

Music's time-line warped
by clinging vines of wind
drawn taut round dusk's waist
beneath raven wings as iridescent crests
of sadness beyond the horizon
touching jagged slopes of silver artifacts
those malleable clouds set against
lavender & grey moonlit skies . . .

dog-eared sweat on God's furled brow
— Old Vienna —
filthy with petty intrigue & squandered joys
conspired with elegant poverty
faithfully attended by genius' tenterhooks
immortality fumbled day to day machinations
as inspiration cascaded like unkempt hair
with fate reckless virago
enhancing wild novitiate verve
as measured beauty from human rote /

Those musical impressions like greedy waifs
pleaded for laying on of hands
when desperate moments coaxed colors
to explode long night's heroic tempest
rabbit for heart and wine flowed
from trauma's fractured reality
streaming anaemic blood
urged to greater heights by self doubt /

Detailed sky full of yellow mums
golden mouthed dawn's bohemian dowry
whose goosebumped timbre wedded sedition
this living myth locked to inner core;
perfection attained through creative deluge
Mozart's brilliance telescoped to wit's end
with life shorter than urgent truth . . .

Raven flight as windward catechism
to life's blazing apocalyptic tear
perdition & burned off question's essence
morning fog caressing unmarked grave

Mozart's miracle challenged
the human capacity for the sublime
& created a universe
indelibly tattooed with superlatives !

DOMINION
FOR DYLAN THOMAS

Disheveled gypsy among notebooks
the boathouse stands its defiant vigil
touch the dream wave spun from gluttonous fervor
catch-phrase the wonder-gleam
curly hair little man of our most persistent fears

Fanned by blue flames
the agony of a poem's line
chipped from the stone draught
of nightmares chasing skeletons
behind the glimmer
of your mischievous bright eyes
as narcisistic pools /

Wanting to believe laughter's myth
cronies refused to notice your loneliness
chanting like a druid bard
among swamp strewn places
where bread crumbs flew from your pockets
full blown herons . . .
when the plump night is quiet and fatigued
with star glazed weight
one can almost hear the belch of maggots
ascending from the dung heap of life long poverty
like a fog of willful manslaughter
surrounding profits you will never see Dylan /

Listen carefully and one may almost hear elements
bruised by circling gulls wings of snow
that flirt with gloaming's whisper
as the moon becomes a bitter pill
against the stellar mirror of blustery wind
pap of nature
perch of erection
nimbus of itinerant peace
where are the cobwebs removed
from the sacrament of flight
where is the Earth ?

COGITO
FOR DANIEL BERRIGAN

To know the temporal beauty of wisdom within
the bombed out church of the soul's civil war
where lines of severe grace are etched
by prehensile sedition in his eyes
like a roadmap toward interdiction

& supple truth's conspiracy gusts
against current events' pin-wheel
as hirsute theatre of the absurd
the only path to justice in america /

Beatific in his sacrifice — free fall gliding
the body frail & battered — life's journey
always harder than it has to be & never long enough

slender templar flesh fashioned into willow-switch
when the empire's infrastructure of rusty steel
expands into freedom's myth
hewn from "Strangelove" lunacy
the hour at hand &
Daniel prepares for yet another battle
to dispel Revelation's prophecy
when humankind covets extinction . . . STAT . . .

A man lives
a man dies
if he is lucky he has been noble
whose hand reaches for the baton ?

THE CALLING
FOR OSIP MANDALSTAM

Mandalstam as uprooted tree
whose unearthed roots are rolled
into cat-o-nine-tails
that spits acid the color
of bloody calculus flying in the head
excreta of candle's tongue
as poetic line walking razor edge
dramatic tension and conscript for exile or tomb
      the song
      the song
rampant for fleet moment calls on specter army
to rise from forest of martyr's gravesites
the nightmare in Stalin's madness
as stiff necked idiom of state
the lingual treason which murders poets
with their frail seditious steps

fashioned into crystal cossacks
that ride winter's stallion breath
of wild balalaika replenished
music becomes rubric musk of memory
that escapes through a window
thrown open as wide as God's eye /

To live
to suffer
to achieve
gambit of the written word
so what remains is who will sing for the poet ?

music
music
music
music — please not this flatted fifth note
dented beyond pawning) for who would come
to buy this solitude then ?

The danger of the waltz
is not believing the whirlwind
the hidden laughter of agony
that courts the taste of brass !

Having already known death
he fears only the absurd weight of loneliness
the poet's song is a tattoo of acid
spume of enraged blood that absorbs
society's pain in a frenetic garden of conscience

the poet's lung filled with miasmic sting
of rebirth ratified by presence of yet another poem
blood flecked yolk of life's golden half circle
that haunts the treason of security
for nothing matters — not the fully empowered season
of the heart's breakdown
nor the industry of preference /

The poet's emotions in hot pursuit of clarity
and this autumn chill is surely dread !
Who will sing of the pit in one's stomach
where nothing touches Earth
eddy of stone that howls like a wolf
within broken latitudes of elliptical frost
that frozen tundra of the spotlight's glare ?

There is no better purpose
than to war with perverse trembling of fraud
in the back-country of the poet's affliction

so what remains
who will sing for the poet ?

TEA WITH POE

Symmetry of reckless contradictions
as paradigm for conflicts' hail
attracted to
perigee of illusion astral projected
into time spiraling like opium smoke
giddy fire churning through neon veins
& hallucination
takes him 100 years into the future

to my table in a coffee house
on the street where he lived
defying death by spectral joy
carved figure from swirling pigments' melange
Poe / midnight mystic
dealing on eternity as hobby-horse hell
this urban fit of fierce sadness

lyric ball & chain of pen / ink
torch-song whispering voice
posed visitor's quandary
his the higher mind sorts time & place
with memory of sienna tinted photographs

Poet's muster as communion
entreats muse forming bond
he & I an energy
drawn from romantic tradition

2nd chance
this forced incarnation
the price for afterlife
his craft more than fantasy / escape

he surveys
upper westside's subterfuge
with nightshade vision
& demurs

the present is prison sentence
for him but literature lives forever
"will" dissolves image
as he returns to self singular & space

his smile of irony my inheritance

THE BLUESMAN
FOR STERLING BROWN

Jim Crow pecking at crumbs
from the breadline's drama
when midnight stalks the poet as hero
spotlight . . . it's showtime !
Man silhouetted against a brick wall
drenched in a moonlit season
that sends a single spike of sweat
to carry worksong's sweltering cadence
with guitar chords laying steel during hard times

and tracks of roadside dust curl
like cigar smoke
and that big legged gal
appears as ghost in thick country air /

Sapphire night stride & renegade
word wisp as web of legend
vantage ease premise calling in a blues minor
oh touch the evening scale
proper like freedom and the open road

yet
and
still

the nature of a traveling man
is to tell big lies & love pretty women
-warm the people Sterling-
roustabout style
ash can fire & woodgrain hooch
in the juke rhythm of a black bottom mystery /

Not forgotten — my man — hell naw
brass nuts don't make it easy
but just think
what life would be
without the weight !

IMPRESSIONS
FOR DEREK WALCOTT

A penal colony of consciousness
cast in the role of island
stranded in mercurial waters of a matriarchal moan
walled up behind beckoning swollen lips
of whorish laughter . . . lascivious and nocturnal

the Caribbean quick with a spawn of sublime pestilence
for the all the syphilitic sores shipwrecked
against the wind's flutter & intertwined
in a mango tree fretwork of a would-be independence
this man —
a contradiction — never mind — truth may come yet
a beggar /

A man almost 44 call him traveler
him having been driven through hot-hot coals
his grey dolphin eyes swim upstream
through volcanic mist wrought into sandy promontory
a face that darts across a carpet of granulated salt water

and him —
an island hoisted up on fleshy stilts
as a flood of infidelities course underneath
consumption awaits survival —
deceiving bastard that he is
no matter — we must play the cards the way they are
dealt /

And people being what they are
given to vocalizing their fear of heights
in a form as the shape and force of certain tides

that flow against the roof of his mouth
and the cliff of his soul
and people have been known to:

discourage honesty
alienate warriors
absorb venom from the cutting edge of mediocrity /

Life may not be a political manifesto
and truth may be just a smile
and the poet's tongue on the succulent orifice of dawn !

MAGIQUE
FOR AIME CESAIRE

An effleurage of magnificent longings
preserved by leeward scent of tropical designs
dwelling within compassion's masterstroke
he is Jesuit of redemption's war;
sorcerer with speech born from flight
of gyring tongues of the balisier

that litigate welts of crippled verbs
whose marrow of foraging lava sweep the Earth
with the mystery of denotation seduced
by incandescence fiery as sun
contracted of copper pox /

With Cesairé's miraculous touch
the hood of petulance peels back
to expose a succulent bandoleer of contraband fruit
bereaved of a weft of stolen possibilities
hidden by the working class' skull queen
perennial ghost of slaughtered harvest
whose feet of whistling birds flock
toward nuance set to assuage
hurtling chaos of colonial law

as pride of tornadoes that maraud
just beneath skin's surface
erupting into true grief
as blue as sounds of dawn breaking

into discordant harmonies of vengeful lust
where aftershocks are engendered by nations
held for ransome
and stenciled across I.M.F. latitudes /

This nuptial garter of islands
plucked from the sea's pulp
by primal force as liturgy of import deficits
classic greed taken a step too far
this duty free terror where the masses
are given to riot; missed meal cramps;
and cathartic madness . . .
between unbearable suffering and remedy
there are actions . . . but first come words !

Effleurage, French, elongated breath, a sigh

Balisier. A wild plantain found in the forests of Martinique. It has a
bright red flower. For some it is like an open heart, while for others, it
represents the flame of revolution

Copper Pox, Caribbean folklore, a venereal disease contracted while
copulating with a woman who sucks on a copper penny during
the sex act.

SEPTEMBER REQUIEM
FOR PABLO NERUDA

No more to feel the spume of humanity's waves
breaking against La Isla Negra my friend Pablo
you are with me for I have learned to measure
loneliness
by the way my footsteps fall on the ear of Autumn
this pus ridden ulcer which refuses to heal
becomes your absence /

The night assaulted weeps with your torture
if I had tears left they would be a bitter wine
poured in honor of your soul all pure and safe
in the womb of revolution /

Oh my brother — to have been martyred by thieves
stealing dreams
where opaline nova light fragments against yanqui deceit

Oh my brother — a great dust has risen from your body
the recollection coughs blood
it is important to remember the poet's muse
starving in the beginning
where solitude was tempered by the raving lunatic's
qualified delirium invading holy places
of the political right wing . . . those believed to be
the dollars and cents of it /

Your life immersed in mint laden rain
falling from canopy of sonorous night
and the countryside of Chile
where the canto of the thrush's vigil coos
like pacific waterfall from your words
as the latin soul leaps into the wolf's shadow
hunting

I will place flowers in the sockets of the skull
of your song left here to forever lament
in a voice lost in the flamenco guitarist's climate

My friend Don Pablo
you with a tongue extended into a field
of wild poppies that speak
of the sweat of workers turned into the fuel
for a new order

Your life born of Antarctic silence
at the end of the world
as lashing rain moans your murder /

PERSONALS

TRANSITION PIECE

The camp in a dogfight of wayward temperament
prowls the province of familiar mistakes
where bad women and good bourbon co-exist
in spiteful detente . . . roving badlands of my fate

with Machiavelli hiding in the ink well
a tradition of blissfully ill advised choices
sits like a flock of harpies
marauding the private hell of my isolation

As custom goes for my totem
unclaimed I be
an orphan raised by she-wolf
I learned to cover my tracks
strike & fade

transmogrify at the drop of a hat
into whirlwind rage
the entire span of what occurs
is reduced to rubble — an aura
save rumor — nothing more —

Hacking bronchitis clears a path for me
through daybreak which glimmers
like a pawn broker's shelf of tarnished brass
and I cannot recognize that face
haunted by age's miscegenated tribal scars
frown lines whip-stinging dark rings
that orbit this stranger in the mirror
who stares at me with 38 caliber eyes

What is adjusted to reprisal
— one hour's grace /
not a minute more —
reminds me that knowledge
and romantic cutting edge
have stolen my youth

This blizzard follows me like a frozen tear
reluctant probing of the tundra's streets
I am a wolf howling of a far away moon
prowling pleasant memories' shadow

a fossil here — a seduction there
and my critics addicted to the banal
those relics seek my conversion
"be demure" they say "your imagery is cockstrong
you may even catch a fly with honey yet !"

I know that I should be more disciplined
anyway indecision makes such fine poems
I shall continue to blunder into themes
as much by default as by ideology

knowing nothing of a pimp's protocol
I say poems come from adventure
and the fur lined open oyster
of my lover's brilliance . . .

I claim life
I write !

AVIS

If we can reach past mistakes
and if we should remember when hunger
and insular idealism were more faithful
than our most beautiful mistress —
her lips parted and teasing
with the taste of magnolia wine . . .

then sweat of catharsis need not mean exile
and tonight these sad lines of twilight shadows
could be a walking cane in a rose garden

whose memories are not crusty enemies
but old friends who tell us the truth
against our own better judgement

and if truth be frightening
a polite smile should justify courage
in full view of bitter conflict !

SLEDGE HAMMER BLUES

Maidenhead of molten rock
and the clatter of my teeth
against the moon;

I am lonely and this hammer be truth /

With a flurry of hornets in my veins
I come to you a child of struggle
forgive my childishness — this war
I fight sometimes turns men into boys

but if truth be anything like
the pain that I feel in my loins
whenever you leave — then suffer me
my lonely madness; hold me !

FRESH

In that long ago
my hesitation
like misplaced notes
scored for an off night's
ego flight on cob webbed wings

"Now's the Time !"

Strawberry cat's claws strike
beyond the pale of limitation
blue conjure's purr
this liana limbed feline
belly slinks like willow soft jazz
as I follow the grail
of moist hypnotic lips

Norma Jean's rendering
lovely
to the point of reckless distraction
statuesque joy she
of full moon laughing eyes
where knowledge / beauty / pain
brews into nectar

The accumen of road dust settles
into sculpted personalities
drawing us toward each other

the song something like a brushfire
that waits for confirmation !

THE WATERING
FOR AKUA

Carrion-priest this warring absence
which scatters your voice / incense in my ear
the grimace of anguished passion

I watched you
forgive me I watched —

as I came nearer your flame
so softly now the magic sears
before urgency looks askance
kiss me deeply my darling
lustful dreams wait
for our moist & fecund dance /

COVERT ACTION

I shivered from the glaze
of N.Y.'s wall of lies
and yielded to temptation
I should've called before coming over
a question mark for a cane
to make my way through
the dialectic of divergent roads
as dramatic prelude
to personal baggage which caused us
to sniff each other's water

The mortar of language
filled harsh spaces
during a day to day interdiction of survival
on this mule path of an urban tempest /

Drawn shades against sunlight
the color of winter wheat
the small talk engrossed in political struggle
confused and hectored lust
for the smell of salty sex & urine
plaited like corn silk
in fertile regions of your rounded flesh

such odds there were against this coupling tandem
but why shouldn't there have been
a fierce romanticism which
wizards rainbows against petty obstacles
where autumn winds' troubadour voice
surrounded the starry flicker of evening /

I remember . . .
stripped of clothes & pretense
our bodies compared salt & pepper pigments
tongues pliant in a free fire zone
your farm queen's feet
high in the stirrups of tenderness
as brioche thighs of daydreams
saddled a neon spell bound by dynamic tensions
pumping mortar & pestle rhythms
while we hugged up on each others' poems
and plied the shy advocation
of a east village slow drag
belly to belly rub
like the old folks say,

"a hard head makes a soft ass !"

TANGERINE
FOR ALISON

I want to see your wild hair
trimmed with the sperm of runaway starlight
a thousand years ago & you at the piano
legs agape where the pedals were missing

Your dress made from an ice cream chalet
and night on the threshold
sucking after your realm of hot fudge
with a fanatical sweet tooth /

I have wandered into this fantasy
where Prince Street is a ribbon
tied through your hair
sunshine — call it tangerine
whipped from the embryo's eye

scarlet wound — call it cherry mouth singing
with tambourine tongue
music where the notes fall in quad triple image
chasing sound

. . . so play it again for me pretty woman
that melody which comes in peasant cotton
I have need of your warmth /

A minute's kindness please . . .
where sunshine follows your kiss on my cheek
like a stained glass laughter
playing a thumb piano
off in the candor of tangerine shade
soft like the sequence of sunspots that smile
whenever I see you /

A minute's kindness please . . .
so I can rest in a corner of your life /

EQUINOX
FOR TOKI

Let there be an essential silence
and passion extended into patience
if only for the sake of spring
with lilac in the air like tenderness

Let there be a meridian of laughter
that travels an azure savannah
pirouetting against an atmosphere
infused with calla lilies

Let there be a twelve string guitar melody
frozen into a Yoruba portrait
of shooting baobab roots that ring out
against effulgent winds which speak
through mystery's thick lips
the shadow of your profile /

And if there be
the slightest pretense of sorrow
let a canticle of bells cry for the acreage
of stained glass butterflies

whose wings capture a fox-fire kiss
from a mulatto moon —
and if that is not enough

let me say that I care !

POEM FOR MY LADY or:
THE BLACK WOMAN AT THE POINT
OF PRODUCTION / A SCIENTIFIC
SOCIALIST'S APPROACH

The milkyway's spiral slidingboard
trackless feeling when we clasp-cling
to better penetrate middle core's wisdom
— but men forget —

So here we are-socialism more fragmented
than a wall of fun-house mirrors
radical journals not much more than
jism-splattered exercises in patriarchy —

I seek rapacious passion beyond ideology
where is the woman's touch ?

I absolve myself of the ruthless farce which shuns
that precious other self — more human & wonderful
My Lady be sensual pell-mell production line
of electric heartbeats that rumble in bellowing climax
her personal inventory reads: warrior / comrade
                                friend / peer
                                comrade
                                fuck buddy

Caring for her has made me schizoid
svelte brilliance in her amber flesh be season of bliss
but . . . it's her whip of a mind that's a talisman
against boredom and weakness

or perhaps it's that dyad of nimbus around her eyes
breaklight guiding prayers in smile's direction ?
Opulent hip for pillow
and premise firm tits as solace
when demigod
whose motherload of bullshit rhetoric
operates en passant — disallowing people —

Like by all means
wealth's proper distribution
is an emotional depth of character
which manipulates two personalities
into wayward union of opposites
the material basis for happiness
cannot be whole

without this pretty woman who allows me
to grow with and inside her . . .

which is to say the future can be a loving trip
which is to say also
I just loves me some dialectical brown sugar !

THE MOB

"There they are, get them !"

One step ahead of the gathering storm
we run from the past
of all those anonymous one night stands
coming through the stone age of lonely times
emerging on location
the opening scene for a monster flick
we are the stars

This host as posse
a cast of thousands flock for the execution

"Burn them, they be witches !"

Your dark honey combed eyes
reflect flaming torches of angry villagers
those who'd be involved in high drama of the chase
not caring at all for our loving ways
wherever we go cynical hordes
hound us with disdain
giving greater definition to
"if looks could kill !"

"Stone them !"

Our racing hearts
sing prelude to the big scene
we duck into subway catacombs seeking shelter
but they still pursue

bitchy rivals swarm around us after the fact
picking at each of our peccadillos like harpies
bushwhacking the good guys and jumping claims

but we are twins of the soul
much stronger than our combined weight
as the wagons circle we fight them off
gaining precious time . . . a quickie perhaps . . .

stay tuned for the next episode !

FIRE ISLAND

A different method of caring
bonded that Saturday odyssey
kindred spirits weighted down
bags bristling with manuscripts
we looked like gypsies
direct from central casting —
Black pearls formed around urban torment
in retreat from dispassionate colleagues
or disloyal playmates
we needed to be alone

seeking peace & quiet
we abandoned N.Y.'s competitive curse
movie cameras capturing angles
from a two-shot lustre
while railroad's rattle threw snake-eyes

the destination your surprise
I willingly followed
waiting on pleasure's sweet reprise

Close to the fragrance of sex about the sea
the boat bobbing up & down
like festive apple — the game afoot
the ferry ride to Davis Park
idle with nascent wonder
of the sea's salt stained welkin
its languorous bodice chameleon shifting
grey
and green

our faces pivoted toward the sun in prayer
our brainwaves
short circuited into fragments of lightning
painted across
curtains of wind & clouds
that rippled like banners
while mare's tails whipped rainbows /

Settled like alluvial silt
in a bungalow buried
by pine cones and primeval scents
we set out adventuring island treasures
walking brown sugar sands
and dropping purple stones
to show us the way back home
our imagination crazed gull soared
through the cottage industry
of solitude and paired laughter

my nutmeg switch
the taste of wine on your lips
while
starlight cascaded over possibilities
& moonrisen purview drew fever out

The music of your breath on flickering candlelight
is what I listen for when I dream
and it be the necessity for dreams
that leads men toward the women they love

Happiness is memories of this week-end
reincarnated by your merry laughter
a place untouched in my heart
something like a jazz ballad
poured into the midnight blue maze
of emotional questing: eternal and satin soft
as a deep kiss speaking in tongues !

SUNDAY EXCURSION

Inspiration from renegade plexus
brought us to a state of grace
special moments' flash-point
bound up tight in the shame faced
drama of "can't get enough baby !"
your body-vale invited exploration
where isobars of entwined limbs
charted lustful marathon
shadow-take on musk stained latitudes
rubbing-stones of sandalwood flesh
and luscious titty muscle
candlelight liqueur samba-beaming
from plump mahogany nipples like tassels /

Sensory re-take
on sweltering heat
that peeled niche around us
laying side by side
X shape sculptures
set in hurricane's eye
my hand cradled your foot
as we rocked in pagan ceremony
passion's grand protocol
demanding another kind of style

I remember our bodies
caught in velvet throes of tender fury
and we were all there was in the world
two different heartbeats
merging into reflective sensuality
I remember the drought of our thirst
never wanting to be without you close

and this is only nomadic love song
following us across the golden moon
may air turn to stardust
as it slips through our clasped fingers
and the magic of that day
be ours forever !

NEW YORK FUGUE

I

Violins and cellos in fervent consort
construct a conduit for us to cross
where brimstone bangles clatter wild praise songs
to our spirits which cartwheel the ozone
we travel the way of a new world
sonic bursts to truth lashing all non-believers

brittle air laden with small puffs of breath
polished jeweled facets in our morning stroll
I smoked a corncob pipe
and pretended not to be dazzled
by the delicious musk of your acumen . . .

giggling as if much younger
we sat among volcanic rocks & evergreen trees
and black strokes on the page
became squawking raven that punctuated
white madras clouds in a blue cobalt sky /

We are heirs to the honor of righteous battle
we be lovers and word masons
laser tongue branding irons
as we chose the method of our enemies' chastisement . . .

you and I simply — a woman —
                            — and man —
bound by quiet thunder in the covenant
between primeval romance of thought
and common laughter of cogent language

which enjoins heady passions to destroy
all nonsense and vainglorious mediocrity

God Bless Us !

II

Gypsy wunderkind whose skin
is an impatient roadmap
in headlong flight from the urban atrocity
of unclean profits and familiar injustice

you have lived the blissful adventure
guided by azure bardic circles
which surround the pupils of your eyes

you are lure of exotic pleasures
that offer safe passage — but for those
unable to absorb the flow of your aura
there comes that emptiness about their mind's eye
where the simoon of your tender mercies scorch &
kindle

but on the other hand . . .

a louma crane's six storied tight shot
captures the form in
your lollipop bodice of cream liqueur
feline-slinking beneath a canopy of tropic heat
— sweet persona of moist & radiant succor —
while dapple sunshine chases a ribbon of music
nuance weaves between bars of shadows & textures /

Louma crane. Device used in the making of motion picures to get
shots of the ground from high vantage point.

Sweet baby . . . you are focused energy
so compassionate & willing
to whirlwind sweep
with new broom's invective
shocking reality into dream / glitter
& a chance for something different

who are you ?
On rare occasions I think that I know
the least of it
someone to cherish . . . you figure ?

III

Pages pleated with masturbation
of poetic lines and I am Peter Pan
swallowed by the fast lane — unable to keep up —
with this broken dominant chord dangling by a hair
where my steps dance among raindrops' voices

Trapped inside of me — from another time & place
there's the romantic soul of a brooding paladin
noble to the point of being selfish
I loose myself sometimes in a maze
of too many campaigns
this pillar to post questing
attracts anther swollen vision . . .
but warrior's code protects fragile inner core
through tactile gambit
and claw of tom-cat's prerogative
I was never meant to take prisoners /

Succubus my love — a touch more than a distant smile
cause I need to hold something
games mean more than the winning
tell me
why only now
after understanding nothing
do I accept this mystery beyond its solving ?

I beg to inquire out of ignorance
what is this storm that pours my insides out
upside down upon the page ?

IV

Perhaps I could accept my existence
as vagrant child of turned up collar
but couldn't there be calm
as if this martial pain
weren't the only art of expression ?

Just a moment's peace in this dreadful corner
an eye for this hurricane
where everything is equal
and not this blind rage
the inconsolable wreck of my song ?

And yet I sing !
unable to ignore rampaging liabilities
with breath of seasonal slaughter that soars
it could be magic
and this zephyr that whistles irrationally
in the gap between my teeth could be exuberance !

V

As we merge into each others' vernacular
and genocide haunts and plagues
our people's creative source of greatness
may our poems metamorphose into ransomed notes
— the future held up to accounts —

as we take testimony from a weal of wicked events
scoop flesh-pulp from the sky-calabash to make paper
pen in hand — we write with ink of black jade mist
configured from life's meager thread springtime wings
that storm the barricades of furies' steel /

Straight to the bridge !
Concepts who in flock fashion
tremble to walk eggshells carpet
we should take foul propositions
straight to the bridge /

Oh Baby
we have been charged with changeling's mission
and this time around we burn 'em
from the ashes we must phoenix shape / shift
creating frantic and marvelous freedom suites

from discord and blue smoke
cause baby we be conjure /

If we fail to use the alchemy of a robust literature
if we fail to unleash all of the power at our disposal
may our bones melt right from under our flesh
and our souls become fodder in the perpetual hell
where literary hacks control and know all paths
to and through the corridors of power !

— Episode —

A nation of clapping hands at my temples
I grasp for a divining chain of shooting stars
as I cast a fowler's net across the firmament
in dangerous times I toast your epic proportions
with its nubile vanity of wet raffia

with the ascension of gunsmoke in our embrace
the pyrotechnics of lust which inspires greatness
when night
wears sartorial splendor of metallic war-paint
& Saint George rides the dragon

as the world drifts below our continental mass of benthos
lascivious bridge of flesh and sinews
fluid muscles to pelvis-clasp and fission-touch contents
of amber moonlight diffused through breakers
as we swim
our movements chant a precious lullaby rock

we travel like orca on looking-glass seas
powerful & confident in the hunt
Rock Me Baby !

when there is nothing left to hold on to
we must come into ourselves as beggars
when all else fails
there is still tradition
yet there might be a moment
as thick as a marmalade tear
that I could share with you !

NUBIANA

NUBIANA

I

I am phantom
I cannot trace
the sand's steps
across the radial kiss of hemispheres
loneliness is my obeah
a hint of topaz in the sun's eye &
deserts in my heart

There are dried riverbeds
swollen to distended arteries
my blood is cold

This madness which eats me alive
limps like monumental sorrows in search
of tongues to lick invisible wounds
like concrete idols with subway veins
sucking flesh into human form

Obeah, Caribbean, magic

II

The night is cold feeling
I cannot afford the wind's laughter
I will use a silken fog for a blanket
and let the sun slowly
chisel this wasteland away from my eyes
with nubian melodies

I am a wanderer
spun gold daughter of the sun
I only want part of the vision
I don't want to vex my mind's eye;
I have learned to dream between spaces /

so it goes from dawn to dawn
this oasis escapes morning's execution
crystal continent of tears
fingering slender reeds of time
has caught the eye of the sun
and the sun conspires with ambitious winds of fate
to overthrow the gelded throne of morning sky /

III

Sky orisha
sun follows morning
down golden chains
to wash city sinews of brownstones in daylight —
spring blossom cannonade
filament of fresh iron pressed to tongue
celibate anguish of concrete singing
but I believe in cow's breath on roots
I am not a mover of things
I believe in the heart

though some days I'm afraid to look
through ebony rimmed spaces
as sky falls to this clot on the mind

I rub my eyes
it doesn't rain
cause all I have are streets where I'm born
walking lean to wind
shadows of copper face /

Orisha, Yoruba, deity

IV

I walk night's thighs
warming my hands by street lamps
and fire with broken glass grating nerves
and night thoughts caking blood on the wind's lips

I am a wanderer
but loneliness is not relative to modesty
so let me snatch the fig leaf
from the genital eye of spring's coronation
stopping this neon laughter
which sends our griots pissing wine

we can love beyond our capacity for tears

Wisdom of the eye
creased by the touch of earth
let me feel you bone against bone
belly to belly
I have nowhere to go except
your arms /

V

Rising star
I stroke the sun
puddingstone of calabash & brown nipple
on the 20th day
my ear to the sun's navel
I heard the laughter
of emerald & turquoise speckled oceans /

Rising star
archipelago of gold around the waist
a dream of fertility dancing
in a washing of blood in the eye;
I have seen my desire
roll of nubian hips
elongated breasts of morning

I have come to pray in the wind's cathedral /

NOVA

_____

THE MUSE
— PRETTY-BY-NIGHT —

A draft of air stacked into column of massive embers
sears grey woolen clouds in evening to create a stage
of moonbeams where a fulvous sylph attired
in transparent leotards of blazing meteor fragments
& verse
performs arabesques on toe shoes of reticent diction

with fawn perception gesturing a flicker
like soft candlelight
she dazzles the page with fingers
that rhapsodize — full throat nightingales —

and were life not a tightrope
of mixed textures dreams would pivot
from her pen of nectar in the burning time /

With hair of cropped chaparral
this auroral shadow of pecan velvet
wears isobase for stretchmarks
where poems have expanded her flesh into continents

she tests the meaning of survival
transfixed by austere events
shortest distance between two points
is straight line — gentle is the song
so touch the lady clean

when inner space as inquisition
is destroyed by sheer joy
her presence is pacific shimmer-pulsing friendship
when warmth in the hands of envious hacks
is hunted animal

SEASCAPE
FOR BRENDA CUMMINGS-ASHANTI

My taste buds adventure-scan
her magnificent gingerbread thighs & legs
extended like sensuous antennae
where the acrylic movement of night's diction
step dances on a sleepy world
pedant swinging from a coral bough
as the wind's curtain ripples across the sky . . .
Botero chic

The pregnant full moon's kite
flies with its placenta strumming a harp
of nomadic time-lines

while a lone seagull perches on a piece of driftwood
and waves multiply beneath the bow
of a child-vessel skimming embryonic fluids
where dream-scents waft the harbor of my lady's womb
&
civilization as we know it hangs in the balance !

THE NEWBORN
FOR NOVA AKOSUA ASHANTI

Through the cesarian gorge
in your mother's flesh
I threw pomegranate stones at the moon
but wounded evening instead

where the sisal sky's indigo lips
kissed lightning shadowed summer night
when you were born — as I remember it —
an ocean liner walked on its keel
past a shoal of limitations through harbor fog /

Grand Sissonne with old woman's skin
your anvil sounds leap out
when least expected — causing milk to leak
from matron starlight . . .

Changeling bundle — so young and yet eager
to grow into a laughter which eliminates everything
but the fantastic dream you'll become one day
everything but your sweet presence in my arms

>   stay safe
>   be happy !

Grand Sissonne. In ballet, a jump into the air from both feet

THE ARENA
FOR MARCUS KWAZI ASHANTI

Put away your knives you assassins
leave him alone — I tell you
he will have his childhood . . .
windchimes of unicorn horns
dangle from the future's eaves
listen little man to the magic
of your youth while you can
     . . . better times for us if we struggle
against assigned destiny
son — empath the way
beyond two city's distance between us
the heart displaced by error

my poverty as bacchanal of tears
gridlocked by wayfarer's curse
    — pillar to post —
a spot of bourbon for convivial pause
between paradox of absent father
and desires for the right thing

when icicles of municipal lime green tarnish
hang from contraband memory & urban tragedy
which estranges man from woman
dream from reality . . . oh my son

there's a new god — the soul of intent
fierce and demanding you run
your stride reaching the horizon's edge
when achievement's fire sears your soul

heart / pound
ear / shock
meter / dash-advance
ride the wind's lonely chariot
extend into race memory Marcus
your limbs like a whip against weakness !

THE SEPARATION

This business of denouement
insists story-line warp
into wilful melodrama

Five years — has it been that long ?
With both our dreams invested
you dare use a question mark for a crutch
and I am no better off than I should be
my retaliation throws impotent tantrums
and melancholy uproots good intentions
as my brows furl & knit
around the anger in what you need
and what little I have to offer

White hot passions implode
dividing truth into distinct realities
yours and mine
an unsteady cease-fire in place
with my hair up in grey smoke
and I wish there were air enough to breathe /

It is midnight where I kneel threadbare
before the altar of romanticism's failure
as gentle ghosts of my children's frolic
weave themselves between my every thought
no easy answers inside
this raging archive of sadness
my precious Black dahlias grow up
into loving sanctuary despite my absence

I sit here in this dark hour
the totem of my father has a strange sickness
the tongue twists & spews passive hatreds
they say it has drunk holy water !

I sit here in khaki — my hunger razor sharp
I want to be lean of spirit
but there is dreadful memory
in the pulse of my weapons !

AUTUMN

A rage of distant feelings
simmers in a sabbath of whispering mists
that brush cheeks of hawk faced ghosts

who pluck bridge cables
like a symphony of sitar intertwined
with soprano saxophone dream voice song of the wind
in this jocular time of crimson tassels
hanging from the cat's eye full moon . . .

So wizard the mystery of climate
twisting into martial law
which changes seasons for order
when thunderstones carve fallen leaves
into sacrificial flame and ash —

A shroud for electric crypts
that lean like emaciated sages
when our wisdom trembles for religion /

Autumn with its crispness be the occasion
for truth when Indian Summer is slaughtered
by the first frost's telling secrets
and uprooted oak lay down their lives
to become a carpet of fumaroles for shamen to trod
like saints into heaven

across clouds that race across the sky
in thick brush strokes as reason animates
blues for grays and tempestuous lavender
taunts the warmth of sunrise /

WINTER

Strawboss of faraway legend
my flesh of dust
is rolled into a fist that rattles
against holes in the sky
where birds fly off for the winter

the sun will not hit a lick at a black snake
with insolence of passion bundled against
rarefied air cut like fine crystal

and tree boughs sag with weight of ice
cracking in my arteries
when the last crab apples on the tree react
as brass gong and cymbal /

Deep within the tutelary irony
between justice and principles
a barren country where fools dance
to the torment of sound as wind and fury;
this is my time !

Touch mediate front line crisis
rogue wind with sweaty palms
that comes to bless afternoons
with peace in the middle of me
the chill more pronounced
than Earth broken by big city dreams
and tomorrow will mend with small decisions
walking on feet of combustible fumes /

Winter is a class action suite against weakness
and I a defendant — throw myself at the mercy
of the elements — my collar up in frigid recognition
Of what must be done /

ON THE ROAD

The wind and I hitch-hiking across upstate New York
while telephone poles paced restless landscape
as grand protocol beyond human pretense
aided and abetted by nature's gossip
summoning an indictment against petty rumbling
of commerce endowed by the local inn

This silent drama in the round
flourishing until the success of wanderlust imagery
is surrounded by a colloquy of wood and fauna
enticed by randy musk of damp moss
air taunt with frost caressing
hard Earth and those small things
which could not retreat from frosty pandemonium /

Overhead
a wedding gown of linen clouds is soiled
by flying wedges that ply their trade
against the welkin of migration's appointment
commonwealth of birds riding autumn gales
whistling past ones ear
like a symphony of wailing kettles'
mocking laughter which punctuates poetry of flight

On the ground
fragile bodies and feathers tremble with cold
and sweetest seven note trill be half penny nail
hedging against hunger — and for briefest moment
the aesthetic of flying seems remote
yet they ritual strut and preen before the lake's mirror

without warning invisible fingers turned the sky's spigot
as currents of beige, white, and grey wings
created wild caesuras across the page of a random fresco
vivid alloy of rust and amber bouillon with jade inlay /

Twilight's skirmish line advanced
with an ounce of pride
and the death of innocence
how long this grief of pewtered sky
endless against rustic mosaic
like man's youth bankrupt
and drawn to disappointment
here in the woods where things really matter
the human touch is superfluous

Shame faced at perverse curiosity about something
calmly greater than dreams and softer than a kiss
I started back home toward
the city as my own wildness
leaving God the better of choices !

THE BANK STREET PIER

Poet as challenge and creative spark
in life and death struggle personified
on deserted wharf rotting with salt spray

the weight from phantom cargoes
leaning to buffeting winds and sea gulls bump the hour
like so many high flying kites attached to meaning
by the sky's laugh lines for veins

"And where was that corner,"
he accuses, "the one I turned which refuses
to accumulate promise but holds all secrets ?"

The Poet as challenge
man as outlaw walking worm eaten wood
which crackles underfoot
like flames from another life —
maritime sweep in conquest of the mind's muddy waters
while the Hudson River jostles the shore
like master pick-pocket
backbone against profit

Outlaw as icon for near greatness
and peddle-point
of conjured
gin & paper cup prophecy
set in meter of robust defiance /

Jitterbug streak & youthful remembrance
strokes the canvas pleading "give me back

the legend of peg legged pants and Savoy step
of high brown splendor !"

When just four bottles of wine in the ice box
and a fist full of poems
stood against a caste system of seasons
an ancient tease moults to dry-fuck patience
grey overcoat and porcelain smoke for cloud
as mare's tail that whisks the N.Y. skyline

which frames a gypsy tide
this pain that turns entrails to jelly
so proctor experience set loose in breakers
along the grain of the river's running wound
to foment tempo /

When the poet as outlaw walks the byway
and system of fable in the flesh
to lift events with hands of sienna crystal
to swaddle hard times in white linen
to be buried at sea

no money
no woman that understands

And the river's waves clamor like applause
free form maneuvers satisfaction
from a treaty of silent longing

as the taste of salt
surrounds each poem's line with triumph !